GREAT
SCIENTISTS & INVENTORS

Henry Ford

by Emily James

Pebble® Plus

CAPSTONE PRESS
a capstone imprint

Pebble Plus is published by Capstone Press,
1710 Roe Crest Drive, North Mankato, Minnesota 56003
www.mycapstone.com

Library of Congress Cataloging-in-Publication Data
Names: James, Emily, 1983– author.
Title: Henry Ford / by Emily James.
Description: North Mankato, Minnesota : Capstone Press, [2017] | Series:
Pebble plus. Great scientists and inventors. | Includes bibliographical references and index. |
Audience: Ages 4–8. | Audience: Grades K to 3.
Identifiers: LCCN 2016023850| ISBN 9781515738800 (library binding) |
ISBN 9781515738862 (pbk.) | ISBN 9781515739043 (ebook pdf)
Subjects: LCSH: Ford, Henry, 1863–1947—Juvenile literature. | Automobile engineers—United
States—Biography—Juvenile literature. | Industrialists—United States—Biography—Juvenile
literature. | Automobile industry and trade—United States—Juvenile literature.
Classification: LCC TL140.F6 J36 2017 | DDC 338.7/629222092 [B] —dc23
LC record available at https://lccn.loc.gov/2016023850

Editorial Credits

Jaclyn Jaycox and Michelle Hasselius, editors; Jennifer Bergstrom, designer;
Jo Miller, media researcher; Steve Walker, production specialist

Photo Credits

Bridgeman Images: Private Collection/Archives Charmet, 17; Getty Images: Archive Photos/
Hulton Archive, 5, Hulton Archive, 15; Newscom: akg-images, 11, 13, Everett Collection, 7, 9,
Heritage Images/Oxford Science Archive, cover, 1, 21; Science Source, 19

Design Elements: Shutterstock: aliraspberry, Charts and BG, mangpor2004, Ron and Joe,
sumkinn, Yurii Andreichyn

Note to Parents and Teachers

The Great Scientists and Inventors set supports national curriculum standards for
social studies related to people, places, and culture. This book describes and illustrates
the life of Henry Ford. The images support early readers in understanding the text.
The repetition of words and phrases helps early readers learn new words. This book
also introduces early readers to subject-specific vocabulary words, which are defined
in the Glossary section. Early readers may need assistance to read some words and to
use the Table of Contents, Glossary, Read More, Internet Sites, Critical Thinking Using
the Common Core, and Index sections of the book.

Printed and bound in China.

PO7886LEOS17

Table of Contents

EARLY YEARS

Henry Ford was born in 1863.
He lived on a farm with his
family in Dearborn, Michigan.
As a child Henry liked to study
farm machines and tools.

Henry at age 3

When Henry was 17, he
moved to Detroit, Michigan.
He learned about engines.
Henry wanted to invent
a horseless carriage.

Henry riding a tractor
he invented

EARLY WORK

In 1888 Henry married Clara Bryant. She believed in his ideas. Henry built a small gas engine. The engine would make his car move.

Clara in 1915

Henry built his first car in 1896.

He called it the Quadricycle.

The car moved on four wire

wheels and had two speeds.

It could not go backward.

the Quadricycle

FORD MOTOR COMPANY

In 1903 Henry started a car
factory. It was called the Ford
Motor Company. In 1914
workers started making
Model T cars at the factory.

Ford Motor Company in the early 1900s

Model T cars were popular because they didn't cost as much as other cars at the time. Many people bought them.

Henry was the first to use an assembly line to make cars. A moving belt carried cars to workers who added parts. The factory made cars quickly.

LIFE'S WORK

The Ford Motor Company

became the biggest car factory

in the world. Henry made cars

faster and safer. He hired the best

workers and paid them well.

Workers made cars at the Ford Motor Company in 1913.

Henry died on April 7, 1947.
His ideas changed how people
made cars. Henry made it
possible for many people
to own cars.

Glossary

assembly line—an arrangement of workers in a factory; work passes from one person to the next person until the job is done; moving belts bring cars and car parts to assembly line workers at car factories

carriage—a vehicle with wheels that is usually pulled by horses

company—a business that makes or sells goods or services

engine—a machine that makes the power needed to move something

factory—the place where a product, such as a car, is made

invent—to think up and make something new

Model T—a car made by the Ford Motor Company from 1908 to 1927

Read More

Baxter, Roberta. *The First Cars. Famous Firsts.* North Mankato, Minn.: Capstone Press, 2015.

Gregory, Josh. *Henry Ford: Father of the Auto Industry.* A True Book. New York: Children's Press, 2014.

McDowell, Pamela. *Henry Ford.* Icons. New York: AV2 by Weigl, 2014.

Internet Sites

FactHound offers a safe, fun way to find Internet sites related to this book. All of the sites on FactHound have been researched by our staff.

Here's all you do:

Visit *www.facthound.com*

Type in this code: 9781515738800

Super-cool stuff! Check out projects, games and lots more at **www.capstonekids.com**

Critical Thinking Using the Common Core

1. Why were Model T cars popular? (Key Ideas and Details)

2. Look at the photo on page 17. What is happening in this picture? Use the text on page 16 to help you with your answer. (Integration of Knowledge and Ideas)

3. Henry was the first to make cars using an assembly line. What is an assembly line? (Craft and Structure)

Index